Heinz Imhof

Delicious Canapés and Hors d'Oeuvres

# Finger Food

Cookery Editor Sonia Allison

Series Editor Wendy Hobson

foulsham

# Foreword

Teasing and pleasing and utterly enticing – what better way to introduce you to finger foods, those artistic and elegant little mouthfuls of temptation. Savoury, piquant and brilliantly-coloured, they are quite irresistible.

Finger foods are designed to stimulate the appetite for the meal ahead, but they also make an eye-catching splash at any cocktail party, just enough to take the edge off the appetite and add their own charm to the proceedings in an elegant and individual style.

When the theme is extended – and you will see how this has been done as you go through the book – and the food is presented creatively and with precision on carefully-chosen crockery, you have designer-label hors d'oeuvres which can be compared with visual feasts in miniature, innovative and very much in the world of *nouvelle cuisine*.

# Contents

# Whetting the Appetite

Finger foods are designed to whet the appetite, and quantities and presentation are very important if you want to set the right atmosphere for whatever is to follow – be it an elaborate dinner or simply conversation. Here are some guidelines to help you.

# Serving and Presentation

When preparing canapés or other finger foods, allow an average of 4 to 6 per person. Avoid offering too wide a variety, otherwise your guests may be tempted to try one of each and not only spoil your calculations, but also their own appetites for the meal to follow.

Serve the foods attractively on elegant plates, perhaps lined with doileys, and decorate the table with linen napkins folded into swans or waterlilies (for instructions see page 8). The bodies of the swans or centres of the lilies can be filled with little bowls of fresh or dried flowers, or even tiny seasonal fruits. When you are selecting your foods, remember that colour is important when you set out the display, so look for a combination of foods which will look attractive together and really complement one another on your table.

In summer, or in warmer weather, keep the finger foods light in style. Choose, for example, Prawns on Herb Butter, Caviare on Quark Toast, Sole Rolls with Cucumber or Chicken Breast with Oranges. If you want to serve a warm dish, again opt for something fairly light such as Baked Mushroom Caps, Sole Strips in Herb Batter or Beef with Soy and Ginger Sauce.

In winter, opt for a more substantial choice of foods. Smoked Salmon on Horseradish Butter, Goose Breast with Ginger Butter or Turkey Kebabs with Curry Sauce are all delicious choices. Warm dishes are often welcome on a cold evening, and some I particularly recommend are Grilled Oysters with Pepper, Lamb Balls with Roquefort Sauce and Liver Cubes with Sage.

Try to avoid repeating ingredients in the foods, and if you are serving fish as a main course, for example, offer meat and

vegetable hors d'oeuvres.

The drinks you offer with finger foods must also be suitable. Light cocktails, dry white wine, a glass of sparkling wine or Champagne make the best accompaniments; heavier drinks tend to dull the appetite.

## Notes on the Recipes

1 Follow one set of measurements only, do not mix metric and Imperial.
2 Eggs are size 2.
3 Wash fresh produce before preparation.
4 Spoon measurements are level.
5 Adjust seasoning and strongly-flavoured ingredients, such as onions and garlic, to suit your own taste.
6 If you substitute dried for fresh herbs, use only half the amount specified.
7 Preparation times refer to preparation and cooking and are approximate.
8 Kcal and kJs refer to the complete recipe and are approximate.

# Napkin Folding

These two simple napkin-folding techniques can be easily learnt and will really enhance your table presentation. Use large, good quality linen napkins for the best results, or heavy paper napkins.

## The Swan

Spread out a square napkin and cover with an equal-sized piece of foil.

Fold 2 opposite corners together to make a kite shape.

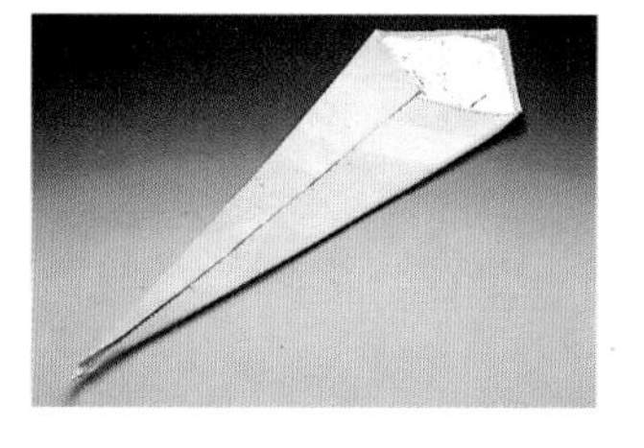

Fold the long edges once again to the centre to make a dart or arrow shape.

Fold the whole arrow lengthways in half.
Take the pointed end and twist into an 's' shaped hook to make the neck.

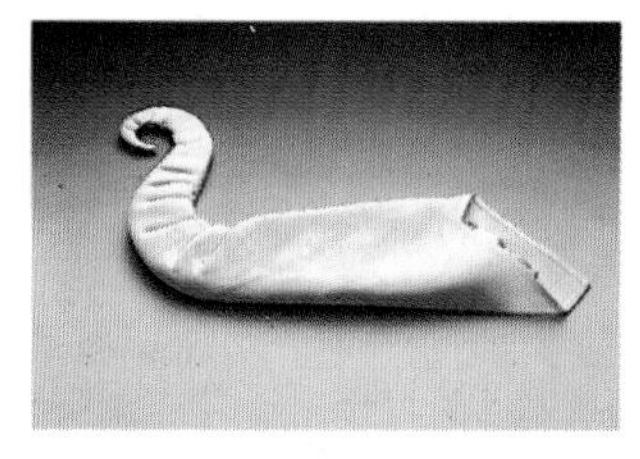

Open out the base of the neck at right angles to form the base and body of the swan.

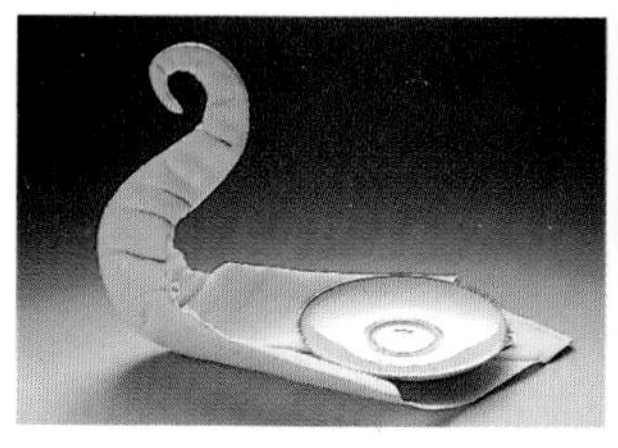

Use a saucer to press the centre section flat.

## The Waterlily

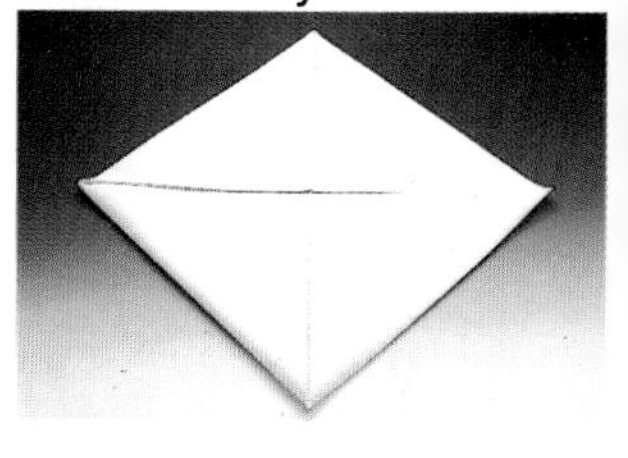

Lay the napkin flat, then fold each corner to the centre and press it flat.

Bring the corners to the centre again, then turn the napkin over.

Fold the corners to the centre a third time.

Place a saucer in the centre to prevent the corners opening up.

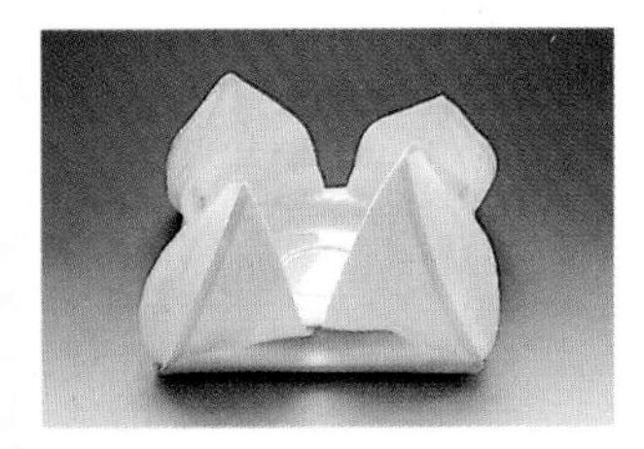

One by one, pull the corners from underneath to form a lily.

# Useful Equipment

**Cutters**: Keep a stock of small and medium assorted-shaped cutters for stamping out bread, toast, potato and other vegetable slices, fruit etc.

**Food Processor**: Not essential, but a food processor or blender will make purées, mixing and mincing much quicker.

**Forcing Bag and Nozzles**: A strong forcing bag with round and star-shaped nozzles in different sizes is used for fillings and decorations.

**Frying Pan**: This is a must for everything that needs frying. A heavy-based pan is best for even distribution of heat.

**Knives**: A small sharp knife is essential for cutting vegetables and fruit, and a medium one for everything else. Poultry shears are helpful for dividing up poultry.

**Palette Knife**: A palette knife or other round-bladed knife can be used for spreading and smoothing things such as butter and cream cheese.

**Rolling Pin**: This is essential for rolling out dough.

**Scales**: Accuracy is important when weighing small amounts, so electronic scales are best.

**Scoops**: A small semi-spherical spoon or melon baller is useful for scooping out little balls, especially of melon, pear or firm pâtés.

**Tartlet Moulds**: Keep a selection of small metal cases in assorted shapes for baking pastry cases.

**Whisk**: Essential for whipping ingredients such as cream and egg whites; a balloon whisk is excellent, but an electric whisk is quicker and less tiring.

**Wooden skewers**: These are useful for spiking food to hold it together or for cooking. They are also ideal for picking up titbits, especially if they are hot.

# Canapés

Most of the canapés which follow have bread as their base and are quite easy to prepare. Different breads have been used to provide a variety of flavours and textures.

*Caviare on Quark Toast, page 12*

# Caviare on Quark Toast

Makes 10
Preparation time: 20 mins
40 kcal/170 kJ

*5 slices white bread*
*45 ml/**3 tbsp** quark*
*10 ml/**2 tsp** chopped fresh chervil*
*20 ml/**4 tsp** milk*
*salt*
*a pinch of cayenne pepper*
*50 g/**2 oz** orange caviar*
*50 g/**2 oz** black or yellow caviar*
*10 sprigs of chervil*

**1** Toast the bread and, using a 4 to 5 cm (1½ to 2 in) cutter, cut out 10 circles.
**2** Mix the quark with the chervil, milk, salt and cayenne pepper.
**3** Spread the quark mixture on to the toasted bread circles and divide the two kinds of caviar, half and half on each. Garnish with sprigs of chervil.

*Photograph page 10*

# Prawns on Herb Butter

Makes 10
Preparation time: 20 mins
90 kcal/380 kJ

*50 g/**2 oz**/¼ cup butter*
*30 ml/**2 tbsp** chopped fresh mixed herbs (basil, sage, thyme, chervil)*
*1 clove garlic, crushed*
*salt and freshly ground white pepper*
*a dash of Worcestershire sauce*
*5 slices white bread*
*¼ lettuce*
*150 g/**15 oz** cooked prawns*
*60 ml/**¼ tbsp** crème fraîche*
*1 tomato, skinned and deseeded and cut into segments*
*10 small basil leaves*

**1** Cream the butter with the herbs, garlic, salt, pepper and Worcestershire sauce.
**2** Using a 4 to 5 cm (1½ to 2 in) diameter round cutter, cut circles out of the bread slices and spread them with the herb butter.
**3** Lay a small lettuce leaf on each and arrange the prawns on top.
**4** Decorate with a spoonful of crème fraîche and a segment of tomato, then place a small basil leaf on top of each.

*Photograph opposite (top)*

# Smoked Salmon on Horseradish Butter

Makes 10
Preparation time: 25 mins
100 kcal/420 kJ

*30 ml/**2 tbsp** grated horseradish*
*40 g/**1½ oz**/3 tbsp butter*
*salt*
*juice of ¼ lemon*
*5 slices of rye bread*
*200 g/**7 oz** smoked salmon, sliced*
*1 peach, cut into segments*
*mustard and cress*

**1** Whip together the horseradish and the butter and season with a little salt and lemon juice.
**2** Using a 4 to 5 cm (1½ to 2 in) round cutter, cut 10 circles from the bread and spread horseradish butter on each.
**3** Twist the salmon slices into rosette shapes and place them on the top. Garnish with peach segments and cress.

*Photograph opposite (bottom)*

# Herring Fillet on Potato Slices

Makes 10
Preparation time: 45 mins
115 kcal/475 kJ

*10 raw potato slices 1 cm (1/2 in) thick*
*30 ml/**2 tbsp** corn or sunflower oil*
*45 ml/**3 tbsp** mayonnaise*
*5 ml/**1 tsp** curry powder*
*salt and freshly ground black pepper*
*2 pickled or salted herring fillets, cut into slivers*
*10 red radicchio, shredded*
*10 orange segments*
*10 sprigs of parsley*

**1** Cut 10 rings from the potato slices and fry both sides for around 5 minutes in oil until golden brown. Leave to cool and dab off excess oil.
**2** Season the mayonnaise with curry powder, salt and pepper and spread three-quarters of it on the potato slices.
**3** Arrange the herring slivers and radicchio decoratively on the potato slices.
**4** Put a dab of the curry mayonnaise on the herring fillets and garnish each canapé with a segment of orange and parsley.

*Photograph (left)*

# Halibut on Tomato Butter

Makes 10
Preparation time: 30 mins
120 kcal/505 kJ

| |
|---|
| *2 tomatoes, skinned and deseeded* |
| *10 ml/**2 tsp** chopped fresh dill* |
| *40 g/**1 1/2 oz**/3 tbsp butter* |
| *salt and freshly ground white pepper* |
| *4 slices wholemeal or nutty bread* |
| *1/4 lettuce* |
| *200 g/**7 oz** smoked halibut, salmon or trout, thinly sliced* |
| *10 sprigs of dill* |

1 Purée one of the tomatoes and cream together with the dill and butter. Season to taste with salt and pepper.
2 Cut the slices of bread into 10 small triangles and spread with the tomato butter.
3 Place a lettuce leaf on each triangle and the fish slices on top.
4 Cut the other tomato into segments and use it to garnish the canapés with tomato segments and sprigs of dill.

*Photograph (right)*

# Trout Fillet with Caviare

Makes 10
Preparation time: 20 mins
80 kcal/335 kJ

*5 slices toast*
*10 ml/**2 tsp** chopped fresh tarragon*
*45 ml/**3 tbsp** mayonnaise*
*½ head of radicchio*
*2 smoked trout fillets*
*40 g/**1½ oz** trout caviare or any other orange-coloured caviare*
*10 tarragon leaves*

**1** Cut each slice of toast diagonally into two. Stir the tarragon into the mayonnaise and spread over the toast.
**2** Separate the radicchio leaves. Arrange on top of toast with the trout fillets.
**3** Garnish the canapés with the caviare and tarragon leaves.

*Photograph opposite (top)*

# Sole Rolls with Cucumber

Makes 10
Preparation time: 60 mins
155 kcal/650 kJ

*120 g/**4½ oz** salmon fillet*
*salt and freshly ground white pepper*
*90 ml/**6 tbsp** double cream*
*5 ml/**1 tsp** pernod*
*4 sole fillets*
*10 ml/**2 tsp** corn or sunflower oil*
*1 l/**1¾ pts**/4¼ cups vegetable stock*
*4 slices sesame seed bread*
*60 ml/**4 tbsp** mayonnaise*
*¼ cucumber, sliced*
*30 g caviare or lumpfish*
*10 chervil leaves*

**1** Chill the salmon fillet, cut it into small pieces, season to taste with salt and pepper and purée in a liquidiser.
**2** Gradually add the cream and continue to mix. Add the Pernod and season the salmon purée again with salt and pepper to taste.
**3** With the skin side upwards, place the sole fillets close together on oiled aluminium foil. Season lightly with salt and pepper.
**4** Spread the fillets with the salmon stuffing and roll up. Close the aluminium foil, twisting the ends shut, and poach for around 20 minutes in the vegetable stock.
**5** Remove the roll from the stock and leave until cold.
**6** Cut 10 circles out of the bread slices and spread with half the mayonnaise. Place a slice of cucumber on each and spread the remaining mayonnaise on top.
**7** Cut the cooled rolls of sole into slices and arrange on top of the pieces of bread. Garnish each canapé with caviare and a sprig of chervil.

*Photograph opposite (bottom)*

**Gourmet Tip**
You can easily make vegetable stock yourself. Take 1 kg/2 lbs of mixed vegetables, add seasoning and bring to the boil in 1 l/1¾ pts/4¼ cups of water, letting it simmer for 45 minutes. Strain before using.

## Tartare Circles on Rye Bread

Makes 10
Preparation time: 30 mins
115 kcal/475 kJ

*1 egg yolk*
*20 ml/**2 tsp** chopped onions*
*1 gherkin, chopped*
*10 ml/**2 tsp** chopped capers*
*2 anchovy fillets, chopped*
*salt and freshly ground black pepper*
*5 ml/**1 tsp** paprika*
*10 ml/**2 tsp** olive or sunflower oil*
*10 ml/**2 tsp** brandy*
*250 g/**9 oz** fillet of beef, finely minced*
*3 slices rye bread*
*40 g/1½ **oz**/3 tbsp butter*
*10 small lettuce leaves*
*5 anchovy fillets*
*5 stuffed olives*

1 Mix the egg yolk with all the chopped ingredients and season to taste.
2 Stir in the oil, brandy and beef and season again to taste.
3 Cut 10 circles from the bread and spread with butter. Place one lettuce leaf on each circle.
4 Arrange the raw beef tartare on top and, using a knife, score the beef into a lattice pattern.
5 Wrap one anchovy fillet around each of the olives and cut them in half. Place the olive halves on the tartare.

*Photograph opposite (top left)*

## Smoked Ham on Basil Butter

Makes 10
Preparation time: 25 mins
90 kcal/385 kJ

*50 g/**2 oz**/¼ cup butter*
*10 ml/**2 tsp** fresh chopped basil*
*¼ garlic clove, crushed*
*salt and freshly ground black pepper*
*3 slices wholemeal bread*
*½ batavia lettuce*
*10 slices smoked ham fillet*
*5 stuffed green olives, sliced*
*5 black olives, sliced*
*10 basil leaves*

1 Beat the butter with the chopped basil, and garlic and season to taste with salt and pepper.
2 Cut the bread into 10 small rectangles and spread with the butter.
3 Separate the batavia leaves and place on top of the bread. Cover with slices of folded smoked ham.
4 Garnish with olive slices and basil leaves.

*Photograph opposite (top right)*

**Gourmet Tip**
You can use any smoked ham for this recipe, such as German lachsschinken, or substitute Parma ham.

## Ham Cones with Soft Cheese

Makes 10
Preparation time: 30 mins
155 kcal/650 kJ

*150 g/**5 oz** soft cream cheese*
*10 ml/**2 tsp** chopped shallots*
*20 ml/**4 tsp** milk*
*2.5 ml/½ **tsp** paprika*
*5 slices dry cured ham*
*3 slices wholemeal or granary bread*
*40 g/1½ **oz**/3 tbsp butter*
*12 small sage leaves*
*2 thin pineapple slices, cut into small pieces*

1 Mix the soft cheese with the shallots, milk and paprika.
2 Cut the slices of ham in half, twist them into cones and fill with most of the soft cheese mixture.
3 Cut the slices of bread into small triangles and spread with butter. Place a sage leaf on each piece and a spoonful of the reserved cheese mixture. Place the ham cones on the top.
4 Garnish with the pineapple slices. Cut the remaining sage leaves into strips and sprinkle on top of the ham cones.

*Photograph opposite (bottom)*

## Roast Beef on Anchovy Butter

Makes 10
Preparation time: 20 mins
195 kcal/815 kJ

---

*½ leek*
*50 g/**2 oz**/¼ cup butter*
*5 anchovy fillets, chopped*
*3 slices white or brown bread*
*30 ml/**2 tbsp** mayonnaise*
*10 ml/**2 tsp** chopped fresh chervil*
*10 slices roast beef*
*¼ batavia lettuce*
*1 tomato, skinned, deseeded and cut into segments*
*10 sprigs of chervil*

---

**1** Cook the leek for about 10 minutes in boiling salted water. Drain and cool. Cream the butter and the anchovies.
**2** Cut the slices of bread into 10 small rectangles and spread with the anchovy butter.
**3** Mix the mayonnaise and the chopped chervil. Spread this on to the roast beef slices and roll them up.
**4** Separate the batavia leaves. Arrange them and the roast beef rolls on the bread rectangles. Cut the leek into slices and garnish the canapés with leek medallions, tomato segments and chervil.

*Photograph opposite (top)*

## Goose Breast with Ginger Butter

Makes 10
Preparation time: 20 mins
140 kcal/570 kJ

---

*50 g/**2 oz**/¼ cup butter*
*10 ml/**2 tsp** grated ginger root*
*a pinch of sugar*
*a pinch of salt*
*4 slices white or corn bread*
*½ oak leaf lettuce*
*20 thin slices smoked goose breast*
*¼ mango, cut into segments*
*1 tomato, skinned, deseeded and cut into segments*
*10 sprigs parsley*

---

**1** Cream the butter with the ginger, sugar and salt.
**2** Cut 10 small rings from the bread and spread with the ginger butter.
**3** Separate the lettuce leaves and place them on the rings of bread. Arrange two slices of goose breast on top of each.
**4** Garnish the canapés with the mango and tomato segments and place a parsley sprig on each.

*Photograph opposite (centre)*

## Chicken Breast with Oranges

Makes 10
Preparation time: 35 mins
120 kcal/520 kJ

---

*2 boned chicken breasts*
*salt and freshly ground white pepper*
*10 ml/**2 tsp** corn oil*
*1 red pepper, halved*
*45 ml/**3 tbsp** mayonnaise*
*4 slices white bread*
*10 round lettuce leaves*
*10 orange segments*

---

**1** Preheat the oven to 220°C/425°F/gas mark 7. Season the chicken and place in a roasting tin. Brush with oil and bake for 8 minutes.
**2** Add the pepper halves and bake for a further 15 minutes. Remove from the oven and leave to cool.
**3** When the pepper is cool enough, remove the skin and slice 10 pieces from the flesh.
**4** Purée the remaining pepper and mix it with the mayonnaise. Cut 10 small rounds from the bread and spread with half the paprika mayonnaise. Lay a lettuce leaf on each round.
**5** Cut the chicken diagonally into slices and place on the rounds. Spread with the remaining pepper mayonnaise and garnish with the oranges and peppers.

*Photograph opposite (bottom)*

# Breast of Duck with Honey-Lemon Butter

Makes 10
Preparation time: 30 mins
135 kcal/560 kJ

*250 g/**9 oz** breast of duck*
*salt and freshly ground black pepper*
*10 ml/**2 tsp** walnut oil*
*50 g/**2 oz**/¼ cup butter*
*10 ml/**2 tsp** honey*
*grated rind and juice of 1 lemon*
*3 slices granary bread*
*½ radicchio*
*10 walnut halves*
*10 basil leaves*

**1** Season the duck breast with salt and pepper and place skin side down in a roasting tin with the walnut oil. Roast in a preheated oven at 200°C/400°F/gas mark 6 for 12 minutes, turning over half way through cooking. Leave to cool.
**2** Cream the butter with the honey and lemon rind. Season with lemon juice and a pinch of salt.
**3** Spread the bread with half the butter and cut it into 10 rectangles. Arrange radicchio leaves on top.
**4** Cut the duck breast into slices and arrange on the bread. Put a knob of the butter on each one and garnish with the walnuts and the basil leaves.

*Photograph opposite (top)*

# Dillquark Puffs

Makes 10
Preparation time: 25 mins
130 kcal/550 kJ

*60 g/**2½ oz**/½ cup plain strong white flour*
*a pinch of salt*
*150 ml/¼ **pt**/⅔ cup water*
*50 g/**2 oz**/¼ cup butter*
*2 eggs, beaten*
*225 g/**8 oz** quark*
*10 ml/**2 tsp** finely chopped onion*
*10 ml/**2 tsp** finely chopped fresh dill*
*a large pinch of paprika*
*salt and freshly ground white pepper*
*30 ml/**1 tbsp** milk*
*10 small sprigs of dill*

**1** Sift together the flour and salt. Pour the water into a saucepan and add the butter. Slowly bring to a rolling boil.
**2** Add the flour and salt and stir fairly quickly for about 1 to 2 minutes over a medium heat until the mixture forms a ball in the centre of the pan, leaving the sides clean. Leave the paste to cool for 5 minutes.
**3** Gradually beat in the eggs and continue beating until the mixture is smooth, shiny and stands in small peaks when the whisk is lifted out of the pan. Do not overbeat.
**4** Using a forcing bag and a star-shaped nozzle, pipe out 10 rosettes on to a greased baking tray and bake in a preheated oven at 200°C/400°F/gas mark 6 for 15 minutes or until golden brown and puffy. Cool on a wire rack then cut a lid off each puff.
**5** Meanwhile, mix the quark and onion with the dill, paprika, salt and pepper. If the quark is too stiff add a little milk. Using a forcing bag and a round nozzle, fill the puffs with the flavoured quark, then replace the lids at an angle and garnish with a sprig of dill.

*Photograph opposite (bottom)*

# Appetisers

These are chic little tasters served on small plates at the beginning of a special meal and are both decorative and delicious to eat.

*Celery with Roquefort, page 26*

## Celery with Roquefort

Makes 10
Preparation time: 20 mins
70 kcal/290 kJ

*50 g/**2 oz** Roquefort cheese*
*60 g/**2½ oz**/¼ cup butter, softened*
*10 ml/**2 tsp** chopped fresh tarragon*
*6 sticks celery*
*1 tomato, skinned, deseeded and cut into segments*
*10 tarragon leaves*

**1** Mash up the cheese in a bowl. Add the butter and heat to a creamy consistency with the tarragon. Place in the refrigerator.
**2** Cut the celery into 7.5 cm/3 in pieces and cut a sliver off the rounded side so that the celery 'boats' will sit flat on the plate and not tilt sideways.
**3** Remove the cheese mixture from the refrigerator and beat until smooth.
**4** Pipe 3 rosettes of cheese on to each piece of celery and garnish with tomato and tarragon.

*Photograph page 24*

## Cocktail Tomatoes with Basil Quark

Makes 10
Preparation time: 40 mins
15 kcal/60 kJ

*100 g/**4 oz** quark*
*20 ml/**4 tsp** chopped fresh basil*
*½ clove garlic, crushed*
*salt and freshly ground black pepper*
*10 large cocktail tomatoes, blanched, skinned*
*10 small basil leaves*

**1** Beat the quark with the basil and garlic until smooth. Season to taste with salt and pepper.
**2** Carve a cross-shaped cut into the smooth end of the cocktail tomatoes using a small knife.
**3** Cut off the upper third of the tomatoes and reserve for lids. Remove inside fibres and seeds then pipe in the quark mixture.
**4** Replace the lids and garnish with basil leaves.

*Photograph opposite (top)*

## Avocado Cream with Salmon

Makes 10
Preparation time: 50 mins
120 kcal/515 kJ

*1 ripe avocado*
*10 ml/**2 tsp** gelatine*
*30 ml/**2 tbsp** water*
*1 grapefruit*
*salt and freshly ground white pepper*
*10 ml/**2 tsp** white vermouth*
*100 ml/**3½ fl oz**/½ cup double cream, whipped*
*10 small slices smoked salmon*

**1** Peel the avocado and purée. Soften the gelatine for a minute in the water.
**2** Peel the grapefruit, then divide the flesh into segments by cutting in between the pithy membranes. Collect any juice and warm gently with gelatine until melted. Stir the dissolved gelatine into the avocado purée.
**3** Season with salt and pepper and add the vermouth. Fold in the whipped cream and refrigerate for 30 minutes.
**4** Arrange the grapefruit segments with the smoked salmon on small plates. Scoop up the cream with a spoon, previously dipped into hot water, and arrange decoratively on the plates.

*Photograph opposite (bottom)*

# Salmon Balls

Makes 10
Preparation time: 40 mins
120 kcal/500 kJ

---

*300 g/**11 oz** salmon fillet, minced*

*10 ml/**2 tsp** chopped shallots*

*juice of 1/2 lemon*

*salt and freshly ground white pepper*

*150 g/**5 oz** spinach leaves*

*10 walnut halves*

*10 ml/**2 tsp** walnut oil*

*1 red pepper*

*100 ml/**3 1/2 fl oz**/6 1/2 tbsp crème fraîche*

---

**1** Mix the salmon, shallots and lemon juice and season to taste.
**2** Blanch the spinach for 2 minutes in boiling salted water. Dip into cold water, pat dry and fill with salmon. Shape into 10 balls.
**3** Place a walnut half on top of each and brush with a little walnut oil.
**4** Bake the pepper in a preheated oven at 220°C/425°F/gas mark 7 for 15 minutes. Remove the skin and seeds and purée the flesh with 20 ml/4 tsp crème fraîche.
**5** Spoon the purée onto the centres of 10 small plates and put a small mound of the crème fraîche in the middle of each.
**6** Using a skewer, pull the crème fraîche to the edge of the plate in the shape of a star and top with a salmon ball.

*Photograph (left)*

# Tuna with Soy Cubes

Serves 10
Preparation time: 20 mins
95 kcal/400 kJ

*350 g/**12 oz** canned tuna fish fillet, cubed*
*100 g/**4 oz** bean sprouts*
*10 ml/**1 tsp** grated ginger root*
*10 ml/**2 tsp** sesame oil*
*juice of 2 lemons*
*¼ batavia lettuce*
*10 ml/**2 tsp** soy sauce*

**1** Place the tuna cubes in the refrigerator. Toss the bean sprouts with the ginger, sesame oil and lemon juice.
**2** Separate the batavia leaves and place one on each of 10 small plates.
**3** Divide the bean sprouts between the plates, put two tuna cubes on each and sprinkle with soy sauce.

*Photograph (right)*

**Gourmet Tip**
If cooked fish is preferred, steam or poach the cubed tuna in a little vegetable stock until just tender. Do not overcook as the fish might break up.

## Herring Tartare with Beetroot

Serves 10
Preparation time: 20 mins
145 kcal/605 kJ

- *1 cooked beetroot*
- *45 ml/**1 tsp** chopped capers*
- *10 ml/**2 tsp** chopped shallots*
- *30 ml/**2 tbsp** chopped fresh dill*
- *1 egg yolk*
- *10 ml/**2 tsp** olive oil*
- *5 raw herring fillets, finely chopped*
- *freshly ground black pepper*
- *10 chicory leaves*
- *150 ml/**1/4 pt**/2/3 cup Greek yoghurt*
- *10 sprigs of dill*

**1** Peel the beetroot and cut two-thirds into small sticks of equal size. Refrigerate. Finely chop up rest of beetroot. Mix with the capers, shallots, half the chopped dill, the egg yolk and the olive oil.
**2** Add the herring fillets to the beetroot mixture. Season lightly with a little pepper.
**3** Mix the yoghurt with the remaining chopped dill.
**4** Divide the herring tartare between 10 small plates then garnish with the chicory leaves and the beetroot sticks. Finally add sprigs of dill and a spoonful of dill yoghurt to each.

*Photograph opposite (top)*

## Sole Strips on Orange Segments

Serves 10
Preparation time: 30 mins
50 kcal/210 kJ

- *300 g/**11 oz** sole fillets*
- *10 ml/**2 tsp** chopped shallots*
- *juice of 2 oranges*
- *10 small endive leaves*
- *1 bunch of basil*
- *10 orange segments*
- *50 g/**2 oz**/1/4 cup butter, cut into small pieces*
- *salt and freshly ground white pepper*
- *a pinch of cayenne pepper*

**1** Cut the sole fillets into 20 strips and place them in a shallow frying pan with the shallots. Pour on the orange juice, cover and steam over a low heat for about 2 minutes but do not allow the liquid to boil.
**2** Meanwhile arrange the endive leaves on 10 plates, adding a basil leaf and an orange segment to each.
**3** Take out the sole strips, drain and divide between the plates. Let the sauce boil away to half the original amount and then mix in the butter, a piece at a time.
**4** Season to taste with salt, pepper, cayenne pepper and a little chopped basil. Pour the sauce over the fillets and serve.

*Photograph opposite (bottom left)*

## Potato Fishes with Caviare

Serves 10
Preparation time: 30 mins
110 kcal/450 kJ

- *2 large potatoes*
- *salt*
- *25 g/**1 oz**/2 tbsp butter, melted*
- *50 g/**2 oz** sturgeon caviare*
- *50 g/**2 oz** salmon caviare*
- *50 g/**2 oz** trout caviare*
- *150 ml/**1/2 pt**/2/3 cup crème fraîche*
- *10 sprigs of chervil*
- *10 sprigs of dill*
- *10 small basil leaves*

**1** Peel the potatoes and cut them into 1 cm/1/2 in slices. Cut out fish shapes about 4 cm/2 in in size with a fish-shaped cutter and cook in boiling salted water for 10 minutes.
**2** Drain and brush with butter.
**3** Arrange the fish potatoes on small plates and place the various sorts of caviare on top. Add a spoonful of the crème fraîche and garnish with the mixed herb sprigs.

*Photograph opposite (bottom right)*

# Haddock with Paprika

Serves 10
Preparation time: 30 mins
105 kcal/440 kJ

| |
|---|
| *1 small red pepper* |
| *1 small green pepper* |
| *1 small yellow pepper* |
| *25 g/**1 oz**/2 tbsp butter* |
| *a pinch of salt* |
| *300 g/**11 oz** haddock fillets, skinned* |
| *freshly ground black pepper* |
| *15 ml/**1 tsp** plain flour* |
| *45 ml/**3 tbsp** corn or sunflower oil* |
| *paprika* |
| *100 ml/**3½ fl oz**/½ cup soured cream* |

**1** Bake the peppers in a preheated oven at 220°C/425°F/gas mark 7 for 15 minutes. Let cool a little then remove the skins, stalks and seeds.
**2** Cut the flesh into fine strips. Heat the butter in a frying pan then lightly braise the pepper strips. Season with a little salt.
**3** Cut the fish into 10 pieces, season with salt and pepper and toss in the flour. Heat the oil in a frying pan and fry the fish gently for 2 minutes on each side.
**4** Place the pieces of fillet on 10 small plates and arrange the pepper strips on top. Sprinkle with a little paprika around the edge of each plate and top with a spoonful of the soured cream.

*Photograph (left)*

# Smoked Ham Rolls

Serves 10
Preparation time: 20 mins
150 kcal/620 kJ

---

*100 g/**4 oz** pine kernels*
*150 g/**5 oz**/²⁄₃ cup quark*
*10 ml/**2 tsp** chopped fresh lemon balm*
*15 ml/**1 tbsp** nut liqueur*
*salt*
*a pinch of cayenne pepper*
*20 slices smoked ham*
*1 small honeydew or water melon*
*10 lemon balm leaves*

---

**1** Roast the pine kernels in a frying pan until lightly brown then leave to cool.
**2** Put the quark in a bowl with the lemon balm, nut liqueur, salt and cayenne pepper. Stir well together and add most of the pine kernels.
**3** Fill the slices of ham with the quark mixture and roll up. Cut the melon in half, remove the seeds, peel and cut the flesh into segments.
**4** Place the slices of melon and the rolls of ham on 10 plates and garnish with the remaining pine kernels and the lemon balm leaves.

*Photograph (right)*

# Rabbit Liver with Figs

Serves 10
Preparation time: 25 mins
110 kcal/465 kJ

| |
|---|
| *400 g/**14 oz** rabbit livers* |
| *salt and freshly ground black pepper* |
| *50 g/**2 oz**/$^{1}/_{4}$ cup butter* |
| *10 ml/**2 tsp** chopped shallots* |
| *120 ml/**4 fl oz**/$^{1}/_{2}$ cup dry red wine* |
| *5 fresh figs, quartered* |
| *100 g/**4 oz** nasturtium leaves* |

1 Clean the rabbit livers and remove all green parts as these are bitter. Season to taste with salt and pepper.
2 Melt half the butter in a frying pan, add the livers and fry lightly for 3 minutes. Remove from the pan, slice and keep warm. Gently fry the shallots in the same pan, add the wine and boil until reduced by half.
3 Reserve 10 quarters of the figs. Chop the remainder. Add to the pan and boil for about 1 minute. Season with a little salt and pepper. Gradually stir in the remaining butter, a piece at a time.
4 Arrange the liver slices on 10 plates. Add the fig quarters, pour over the fig butter and garnish with the nasturtium leaves.

*Photograph opposite (top)*

# Liver Parfait with Apple

Serves 10
Preparation time: 1 hour
150 kcal/640 kJ

| |
|---|
| *2 apples, peeled, cored and thinly sliced* |
| *150 ml/$^{1}/_{4}$ **pt**/$^{2}/_{3}$ **cup port*** |
| ***15 ml/1 tbsp** gelatine* |
| *45 ml/**3 tbsp** water* |
| *100 g/**4 oz**/$^{1}/_{2}$ cup butter* |
| *150 g/**5 oz** chicken or turkey livers* |
| *salt and freshly ground black pepper* |
| *100 ml/**3$^{1}/_{2}$ fl oz**/$^{1}/_{2}$ cup double cream, whipped* |
| *10 sprigs of chervil* |

1 Place two-thirds of the apples and the port in a saucepan, bring to the boil and simmer gently until the apples are just tender. Do not allow the fruit to overcook as it will break up. Drain, reserving the port, and allow to cool.
2 Soften the gelatine in the water, add the port and dissolve gently over a low heat.
3 Chop the remaining apples. Melt the butter and fry the liver and chopped apple over a low heat for 10 minutes. Season to taste with salt and pepper then leave to cool.
4 Purée the liver mixture in a food processor with one-third of the gelatine mixture. Cover and leave to cool then refrigerate until beginning to set. Pour the remaining jelly into a small dish and leave in the refrigerator to set.
5 Fold the cream into the liver mixture then cover and refrigerate until firm.
6 When the wine jelly has set, tip it on to a piece of damp greaseproof paper and cut it into small cubes using a knife dipped in cold water. Arrange the apple slices and jelly cubes on 10 plates, add a spoonful of the liver parfait and garnish with chervil.

*Photograph opposite (bottom)*

**Gourmet Tip**
For best results, use firm eating apples such as Cox or Granny Smith.

# Quail Breast with Quail Eggs

Serves 10
Preparation time: 40 mins
120 kcal/505 kJ

*5 quails*

*20 ml/**4 tsp** olive oil*

*75 g/**3 oz** carrots, finely chopped*

*75 g/**3 oz** celery, finely chopped*

*10 ml/**2 tsp** chopped shallots*

*1 tomato, skinned and chopped*

*2 sprigs of rosemary*

*150 ml/¼ **pt**/⅔ cup red wine*

*300 ml/½ **pt**/1¼ cups water*

*100 g/**4 oz**/½ cup butter, at room temperature*

*salt and freshly ground black pepper*

*5 boiled quail eggs*

*10 ml/**2 tsp** chopped fresh parsley*

**1** Joint the quails and separate the breast and legs. Brown the carcasses in half the olive oil for about 5 minutes, then add the carrots, celery and shallots. Fry for 5 minutes.

**2** Add the tomato and rosemary. After 3 minutes, pour in the wine and water. Bubble gently until the liquid is reduced to about one third of its original quantity.

**3** Strain mixture into a clean pan. Gradually stir in half the butter, a piece at a time. Reheat gently and season to taste with salt and pepper. Reserve.

**4** Shell and halve the quail eggs. Take out the yolks and mix with remaining butter and parsley. Season to taste with salt and pepper.

**5** Fill the egg whites with the egg yolk mixture and garnish with a little parsley and pieces of tomato.

**6** Season the quail breast and legs with salt and pepper and fry in the remaining olive oil until the flesh is a pinky colour. Allow 5 to 7 minutes. Place on 10 plates, cover with the wine sauce and garnish each with an egg half.

# Breast of Duck with Beansprouts

Serves 10
Preparation time: 40 mins
135 kcal/565 kJ

- *2 boned breasts of duck*
- *salt and freshly ground black pepper*
- *10 ml/***2 tsp** *honey*
- *20 ml/***4 tsp** *olive oil*
- *10 ml/***2 tsp** *butter*
- *15 ml/***1 tbsp** *chopped shallots*
- *1 clove garlic, crushed*
- *150 g/***5 oz** *beansprouts*
- *150 ml/¼* **pt**/*⅔ cup single cream*
- *10 ml/***2 tsp** *chopped fresh chervil*
- *5 ml/***1 tsp** *raspberry vinegar*
- *a pinch of nutmeg*
- *10 sprigs of chervil*

**1** Season the duck breasts to taste with salt and pepper and spread with honey.
**2** Heat the oil in a frying pan, add the duck breasts skin side down and brown quickly, turning twice. Transfer to a roasting tin and roast in a preheated oven at 200°C/400°F/gas mark 6 for 15 minutes. Remove them from the oven, carve into thin slices and keep them warm.
**3** Melt the butter in the same frying pan and fry the shallots and garlic until just beginning to soften. Add the beansprouts and cream and toss together over a low heat for 5 minutes.
**4** Bring to the boil and boil gently until the liquid has reduced by half then stir in the chopped chervil, raspberry vinegar and nutmeg.
**5** Divide the beansprouts, sauce and duck slices between 10 plates and garnish with the chervil.

*Photograph opposite (top)*

# Fillet of Lamb with Aubergine Piccata

Serves 10
Preparation time: 30 mins
150 kcal/630 kJ

- *1 aubergine, sliced*
- *salt and freshly ground black pepper*
- *10 ml/***2 tsp** *plain flour*
- *2 eggs*
- *25 g/***1 oz** *Parmesan cheese, grated*
- *45 ml/***3 tbsp** *olive oil*
- *300 ml/***11 oz** *lamb fillet*
- *10 ml/***2 tsp** *chopped shallots*
- *1 clove garlic, crushed*
- *3 tomatoes, skinned, deseeded and cubed*
- *5 ml/***1 tsp** *chopped fresh oregano*
- *10 sprigs of oregano*

**1** Season the aubergine slices with salt and pepper and toss lightly in flour.
**2** Beat the eggs and mix with the Parmesan. Pass the aubergine slices through this mixture, fry fairly briskly in half of the olive oil until golden brown then keep in a warm place.
**3** Season the fillet of lamb with salt and pepper. Heat the remaining olive oil in a frying pan, add the lamb and fry for about 4 minutes on a low heat – it should remain pink inside – and keep it warm.
**4** Gently fry the shallots and garlic in the remaining oil in the pan. Add the tomatoes to pan with the chopped oregano. Season lightly with salt and pepper.
**5** Cut open the fillet of lamb and arrange, with the aubergine slices, on 10 pre-warmed plates. Garnish with sprigs of oregano.

*Photograph opposite (bottom)*

**Gourmet Tip**
Tomatoes are easy to peel if they are first dipped into boiling water and then immediately into ice-cold water.

# Fillet Slices with Cottage Cheese

Serves 10
Preparation time: 30 mins
55 kcal/230 kJ

*200 g/**7 oz** cottage cheese*
*20 ml/**4 tsp** chopped fresh basil*
*juice of 1 lime*
*salt and freshly ground black pepper*
*225 g/**8 oz** fillet of beef, chilled*
*1 papaya (paw-paw), halved, skinned and deseeded*
*10 basil leaves*

**1** Mix the cottage cheese with the basil and the lime juice and season to taste with salt and pepper.
**2** Cut the fillet of beef into 20 very thin slices.
**3** Lightly season the slices with salt and pepper then fill with the cottage cheese and roll up.
**4** Cut the papaya flesh into segments and arrange, with the fillet rolls, on to 10 plates. Garnish with the basil leaves.

*Photograph (left)*

# Fillet Slices with Olive Vinaigrette

Serves 10
Preparation time: 20 mins
120 kcal/500 kJ

*50 g/**2 oz** black olives, stoned and chopped*
*50 g/**2 oz** green olives, stoned and chopped*
*10 ml/**2 tsp** chopped shallots*
*2.5 ml/**1/2 tsp** prepared mustard*
*2.5 ml/**1/2 tsp** chopped fresh thyme*
*20 ml/**4 tsp** sherry vinegar*
*salt and freshly ground black pepper*
*a pinch of sugar*
*60 ml/**4 tbsp** olive oil*
*10 slices veal fillet*
*10 endive leaves*
*20 black and green olives, stoned*
*10 small sprigs of thyme*

**1** Mix the chopped olives with the shallots, mustard, thyme, and sherry vinegar. Season with salt, pepper and sugar, and stir in one-third of the oil.
**2** Season the veal fillets lightly with salt and pepper. Heat the remaining olive oil in a frying pan and fry the meat for about 1 minute on each side.
**3** Arrange the endive leaves on 10 plates. Add the veal fillet and coat with the olive dressing. Garnish with the remaining olives and the thyme sprigs.

*Photograph (right)*

## Fried Black Sausage

Serves 10
Preparation time: 30 mins
220 kcal/920 kJ

*2 pears*
*25 g/**1 oz**/2 tbsp sugar*
*150 ml/¼ **pt**/⅔ cup dry white wine*
*30 ml/**2 tbsp** vinegar*
*100 g/**4 oz**/½ cup butter*
*225 g/**8 oz** black sausage, skinned*
*½ oak leaf lettuce*
*40 g/**1½ oz** grated horseradish*

**1** Peel the pears and cut into segments. Boil the sugar with the wine until the sugar dissolves then poach the pears in the syrup for 3 minutes.
**2** Remove the pears then boil the juice until reduced by two-thirds. Remove from the heat. Add the vinegar and stir in 75 g/3 oz/⅓ cup of butter.
**3** Cut the black sausage into 10 slices. Heat the remaining butter and lightly fry the sausage for 2 minutes on each side.
**4** Separate the lettuce leaves and divide between 10 plates. Arrange the sausage on top and garnish with pear segments and horseradish. Moisten with the juice in which pears were poached.

*Photograph opposite (top)*

## Stuffed Prunes

Serves 10
Preparation time: 30 mins
350 kcal/1470 kJ

*10 large prunes, stoned and soaked for 30 mins in hot water*
*150 g/**5 oz** minced beef*
*30 ml/**2 tbsp** single cream*
*10 ml/**2 tsp** chopped fresh mint*
*salt and freshly ground black pepper*
*10 rashers streaky bacon*
*10 ml/**2 tsp** chopped shallots*
*2.5 ml/½ **tsp** prepared mustard*
*20 ml/**4 tsp** raspberry vinegar*
*30 ml/**2 tbsp** olive oil*
*225 g/**8 oz** green beans*
*10 endive leaves*

**1** Drain the prunes.
**2** Knead the meat with the cream, mint, salt and pepper and fill the prunes with the mixture.
**3** Wrap each one in a rasher of bacon and hold together with a cocktail stick. Bake in a preheated oven at 200°C/400°F/gas mark 6 for 15 minutes.
**4** Beat the shallots, mustard, vinegar and olive oil then season. Blanch the beans for 3 minutes in boiling salted water and add to the dressing.
**5** Arrange the endive on 10 plates. Add the beans and place the prunes on top.

*Photograph opposite (centre)*

## Stuffed Turnips

Serves 10
Preparation time: 40 mins
160 kcal/655 kJ

*10 small turnips*
*10 ml/**2 tsp** salt*
*1 red pepper, cubed*
*1 aubergine, cubed*
*1 clove garlic, crushed*
*10 ml/**2 tsp** chopped shallots*
*25 g/**1 oz**/2 tbsp butter*
*100 ml/**3½ fl oz**/½ cup dry white wine*
*300 ml/½ **pt**/1½ cups single cream*
*a pinch of saffron strands*
*freshly ground white pepper*
*10 chervil sprigs*

**1** Peel the turnips, cut them flat at the base, cut off a lid at the top and hollow out. Boil them for 10 minutes in salted water.
**2** Fry the pepper, aubergine, garlic and shallots lightly in the butter for 3 minutes.
**3** Add the wine, bring to the boil. Pour in the cream and saffron and simmer for 10 minutes.
**4** Drain turnips, fill the hollows with fried vegetables and top with the lids. Arrange on 10 plates.
**5** Quickly reboil the sauce, season with pepper and pour over the turnips. Garnish with chervil.

*Photograph opposite (bottom)*

# Hot Delicacies

These little tasters lend themselves particularly well to cocktail parties as they provide a welcome alternative to the traditional cold buffet and, served on skewers and without cutlery, are easy to eat.

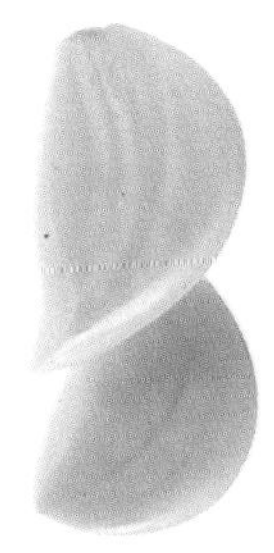

*Baked Mushroom Caps,*
*page 46*

## Baked Mushroom Caps

Makes 10
Preparation time: 15 mins
140 kcal/585 kJ

- *10 large mushrooms*
- *5 ml/**1 tsp** chopped shallots*
- *1 clove garlic, crushed*
- *25 g/**1 oz**/2 tbsp butter*
- *60 ml/**4 tbsp** dry white wine*
- *100 ml/**3½ fl oz**/½ cup cream*
- *3 eggs, separated*
- *salt and freshly ground black pepper*
- *5 ml/**1 tsp** chopped fresh parsley*
- *10 aubergine slices, 2 mm/$^1/_{16}$ **in** thick*
- *30 ml/**2 tbsp** plain flour*
- *50 g/**2 oz**/6 tbsp breadcrumbs*
- *oil for deep frying*

**1** Break off the mushroom stalks and finely chop. Fry the shallots and the garlic lightly in the butter.
**2** Add the chopped mushroom stalks and cook quickly until they have absorbed the butter. Cover with wine and boil until most of it has evaporated.
**3** Pour in half the cream and bring gently to the boil. Whisk the remaining cream with the egg yolks and gradually add to the mushroom mixture, stirring all the time.
**4** Heat gently until the mixture thickens. Remove from heat. Season then stir in the parsley. Leave to cool.
**5** Fill the mushroom caps with the creamy forcemeat and cover with aubergine slices. Season lightly with salt and pepper and sprinkle with flour. Turn in the egg whites then coat with the breadcrumbs.
**6** Fry in hot oil for 5 minutes. Serve hot with a herb-flavoured mayonnaise.

*Photograph page 44*

**Variation**
The mushroom caps can be coated with ground hazel nuts instead of breadcrumbs. This gives them an interesting and unusual flavour.

## Stuffed Courgettes with Prawns

Makes 10
Preparation time: 20 mins
100 kcal/420 kJ

- *1 large courgette*
- *salt and freshly ground white pepper*
- *40 g/**1½ oz**/3 tbsp butter*
- *10 ml/**2 tsp** chopped shallots*
- *1 tomato, skinned, deseeded and chopped*
- *150 ml/¼ **pt**/⅔ cup crème fraîche*
- *225 g/**8 oz** peeled prawns*
- *10 ml/**2 tsp** chopped fresh dill*
- *10 sprigs of dill*

**1** Cut the courgette into 10 thick slices then chop the remainder. Hollow out the centres of the slices using a melon baller and season to taste with salt and pepper.
**2** Heat the butter in a frying pan and cook the courgette slices gently for 2 minutes, turning twice. Remove them from the pan and keep warm.
**3** Add the shallots to the pan and fry gently. Add the chopped courgette and fry for 2 minutes. Add the tomato and crème fraîche and warm through gently but do not allow the mixture to boil. Season to taste with salt and pepper and stir over a low heat for 3 minutes.
**4** Add the prawns and heat through briefly. Use to fill the courgette slices, sprinkle with chopped dill and garnish with dill sprigs.

*Photograph opposite*

# Grilled Oysters with Pepper

Makes 10
Preparation time: 25 mins
135 kcal/565 kJ

---

*10 oysters*

*25 g/**1 oz**/2 tbsp butter*

*10 ml/**2 tsp** chopped shallots*

*1 yellow pepper, chopped*

*100 ml/**3½ fl oz**/½ cup dry white wine*

*150 ml/**¼ pt**/⅔ cup crème fraîche*

*salt and freshly ground black pepper*

*a pinch of cayenne pepper*

*1 egg yolk*

*30 ml/**2 tbsp** double cream, whipped*

*10 ml/**2 tsp** chopped fresh parsley*

*50 g/**2 oz** Parmesan cheese, grated*

---

**1** Open the oysters with a sharp knife, loosen the flesh and remove to a bowl. Clean the shells.
**2** Heat the butter in a saucepan, add the shallots and fry gently for 4 minutes.
**3** Add the pepper and fry for a further 2 minutes. Cover with the wine, bring to the boil and simmer for 3 minutes.
**4** Add the oysters, poach for a few minutes and remove to a plate.
**5** Stir in the crème fraîche and heat gently until the sauce has reduced by half. Season to taste with salt, pepper and cayenne pepper.
**6** Remove the peppers and shallots from the pan with a slotted spoon and place them in the oyster shells. Arrange the oysters on top.
**7** Beat the egg yolk into the cream sauce and heat through without boiling. Fold in the cream, parsley and Parmesan.
**8** Coat the oysters with the sauce and grill until lightly browned.

*Photograph opposite (top)*

# Giant Prawns in Parsley Butter

Makes 10
Preparation time: 20 mins
105 kcal/440 kJ

---

*1 × 225 g/**8 oz** head of celeriac, quartered*

*salt*

*juice of 1 lemon*

*10 large prawns*

*freshly ground black pepper*

*75 g/**3 oz**/⅓ cup butter*

*1 garlic clove, crushed*

*30 ml/**2 tbsp** chopped fresh parsley*

---

**1** Cook the celeriac in boiling salted water with the lemon juice for about 20 minutes until tender. Drain and cut into cubes.
**2** Thread the celeriac alternately with the prawns on to small skewers and season to taste with salt and pepper. Melt half the butter and fry the skewers lightly for 4 minutes, turning frequently. Transfer to serving plates and keep warm.
**3** Melt the remaining butter in the same pan and stir in the garlic and parsley. Cook for 2 minutes then pour over the kebabs and serve.

*Photograph opposite (bottom)*

# Mussels with Leeks

Makes 10
Preparation time: 25 mins
95 kcal/400 kJ

*225 g/**8 oz** leek*

*25 g/**1 oz**/2 tbsp butter*

*250 ml/**8 fl oz**/1 cup crème fraîche*

*salt and freshly ground white pepper*

*a pinch of cayenne pepper*

*1 tomato, skinned, deseeded and chopped*

*10 large mussels of about 5 cm (2 in) diameter*

*10 ml/**2 tsp** chopped fresh parsley*

**1** Cut the leek into 1 cm/½ in cubes, wash and wipe dry. Heat the butter in a pan, add the leek and cook for 3 minutes.
**2** Add the crème fraîche and simmer gently until reduced by half. Season with salt, pepper and cayenne pepper and add the tomato.
**3** Open the mussels. To do this insert a small knife in the side and twist. Discard any mussels which are open.
**4** Lift out the flesh, add to the leeks and let them cook briskly for a moment or two.
**5** Wash out the deep mussel shells and dry. Return the flesh to the shells with the leek mixture and sprinkle with parsley.

*Photograph (top left)*

# Scallop and Courgette Kebabs

Makes 10
Preparation time: 15 mins
70 kcal/295 kJ

| |
|---|
| *300 g/**11 oz** scallops* |
| *1 courgette, cubed* |
| *salt and freshly ground black pepper* |
| *50 g/**2 oz**/¼ cup butter* |
| *1 shallot, chopped* |
| *1 tomato, skinned, deseeded and chopped* |
| *20 ml/**4 tsp** chopped fresh basil* |

**1** Remove the scallops with their corals from the shells, wash thoroughly and cut into cubes. Thread on to skewers alternately with the courgette cubes. Season to taste with salt and pepper.
**2** Heat the butter in a frying pan and fry the kebabs over a medium heat for 4 minutes, turning twice. Transfer to serving plates and keep warm.
**3** Add the shallot to the pan and fry gently until soft. Add the tomato and basil and season to taste with salt and pepper. Heat through for 3 minutes then pour over the kebabs.

*Photograph (right)*

# Sole Medallions with Coconut

Makes 10
Preparation time: 20 mins
160 kcal/665 kJ

- *10 sole medallions*
- *salt and freshly ground white pepper*
- *10 ml/***2 tsp** *plain flour*
- *1 egg, beaten*
- *100 g/***4 oz***/½ cup desiccated coconut*
- *100 ml/***3½ fl oz***/½ cup corn or sunflower oil*
- *1 red pepper, cut into 10 pieces*
- *10 pineapple pieces*
- *juice of 1 lemon*

**1** Season the sole medallions with salt and pepper, toss in flour then coat with beaten egg.
**2** Coat all over with the coconut. Heat the oil in a frying pan, add the fish and fry for 4 minutes over a medium heat, turning twice.
**3** Spear the pepper pieces and pineapple pieces on to cocktail sticks. Add one to each well-drained medallion. Sprinkle with lemon juice and serve.

*Photograph opposite (top)*

# Salmon Tartare on Turnip Slices

Makes 10
Preparation time: 25 mins
115 kcal/475 kJ

- *10 ml/***2 tsp** *chopped shallots*
- *5 ml/***1 tsp** *chopped capers*
- *10 ml/***2 tsp** *chopped fresh parsley*
- *1 egg yolk*
- *juice of ½ lemon*
- *300 g/***11 oz** *salmon fillet, minced*
- *salt and freshly ground black pepper*
- *2 turnips, peeled and sliced*
- *50 g/***2 oz***/¼ cup butter*
- *10 ml/***2 tsp** *olive oil*
- *10 stuffed olives*

**1** Mix the shallots, capers, parsley, egg yolk and lemon juice.
**2** Add the salmon fillet and season with salt and pepper. Knead and shape into 10 balls. Chill for 15 minutes.
**3** Cut the turnip slices into rounds using a biscuit cutter. Blanch the slices in boiling salted water for 5 minutes then wipe dry.
**4** Heat the butter and olive oil in a frying pan, add the salmon balls and fry for 2 to 3 minutes, turning 3 or 4 times.
**5** Drain the salmon balls and place on the turnip slices. Add an olive to each and hold in place with a cocktail stick.

*Photograph opposite (centre)*

# Sole Strips in Herb Batter

Makes 10
Preparation time: 20 mins
155 kcal/650 kJ

- *100 g/***4 oz***/1 cup plain flour*
- *10 ml/***2 tsp** *olive oil*
- *2 eggs, separated*
- *120 ml/***4 fl oz***/½ cup dry white wine*
- *salt and freshly ground white pepper*
- *a pinch of nutmeg*
- *30 ml/***2 tbsp** *chopped mixed fresh herbs (basil, chervil, parsley, dill)*
- *300 g/***11 oz** *sole fillet*
- *oil for deep frying*

**1** Reserve 10 ml/2 tsp of flour. Put the remaining flour into a bowl and gradually beat in the olive oil egg yolks and the wine. Beat until smooth.
**2** Season with salt, pepper and nutmeg. Whisk the egg whites to a stiff snow and gently cut and fold into the batter. Add the herbs.
**3** Cut the sole fillets into 10 strips, season with salt and pepper and toss in the reserved flour.
**4** Coat the sole with the batter and fry in the hot oil for about 5 minutes. Remove from the pan and drain. Serve straight away.

*Photograph opposite (bottom)*

# Turkey Kebabs with Curry Sauce

Makes 10
Preparation time: 20 mins
120 kcal/500 kJ

*300 g/**11 oz** turkey breast, skinned*
*1/4 pineapple, peeled*
*1 red pepper*
*salt and freshly ground black pepper*
*50 g/**2 oz**/1/4 cup butter*
*10 ml/**2 tsp** chopped onion*
*1/2 clove garlic, crushed*
*10 ml/**2 tsp** curry powder*
*150 ml/**1/4 pt**/2/3 cup chicken stock*
*150 ml/**1/4 pt**/2/3 cup cream*

**1** Cut the turkey breast, pineapple and pepper into cubes of equal size. Spear on to 10 smallish skewers or cocktail sticks.
**2** Season the skewers with salt and pepper. Heat the butter in a frying pan, add the skewers and fry until golden brown, turning twice. After about 5 minutes remove, drain and keep warm.
**3** Add the onion and garlic to the pan and fry lightly until just beginning to soften. Add the curry powder and chicken stock.
**4** Boil quickly until reduced by half, stir in the cream and boil steadily until it, too, has reduced to half its original amount. Season with salt and pour over the skewers.

*Photograph opposite (top)*

# Liver Cubes with Sage

Makes 10
Preparation time: 20 mins
120 kcal/500 kJ

*20 ml/**4 tsp** olive oil*
*300 g/**11 oz** calves liver, cut into 10 cubes*
*salt and freshly ground black pepper*
*10 ml/**2 tsp** chopped shallots*
*1 clove garlic, crushed*
*75 g/**3 oz**/1/3 cup butter*
*10 cherry tomatoes, skinned*
*20 ml/**4 tsp** chopped sage*

**1** Heat the oil, add the liver and fry for about 3 minutes, turning twice. The liver should stay pink. Season lightly and keep warm.
**2** Fry the shallots and garlic gently in the butter then add the tomatoes and heat through. Season.
**3** Spear the tomatoes on to skewers with the fried liver cubes. Spoon melted sage butter over each.

*Photograph opposite (bottom left)*

# Veal Sweetbreads with Lime

Makes 10
Preparation time: 30 mins
215 kcal/895 kJ

*350 g/**12 oz** veal sweetbreads*
*3 limes*
*salt and freshly ground black pepper*
*30 ml/**2 tbsp** plain flour*
*1 egg, beaten*
*150 g/**5 oz** fresh breadcrumbs*
*oil for deep frying*
*100 ml/**3 1/2 fl oz**/1/2 cup chicken stock*
*100 ml/**3 1/2 fl oz**/1/2 cup dry white wine*
*150 ml/**1/4 pt**/2/3 cup crème fraîche*

**1** Blanch the sweetbreads in boiling water for 3 minutes. Drain, cover with cold water and leave to cool. Remove the skins then cut into 10 pieces.
**2** Finely grate the rind of 2 limes and squeeze the juice. Peel the third lime and cut into segments. Season the sweetbreads with the juice of 1 lime and salt and pepper to taste.
**3** Coat the sweetbreads in flour then dip in egg and breadcrumbs. Heat the oil and deep-fry the sweetbreads for 5 minutes.
**4** Meanwhile, boil the stock and wine until reduced by half then whisk in the crème fraîche. Cook over a low heat for 2 minutes without boiling.
**5** Add the grated lime rind and remaining lime juice and season to taste. Reheat without boiling.
**6** Spear a cocktail stick into each piece of sweetbread and top with a segment of lime. Serve the sauce separately.

*Photograph opposite (bottom right)*

# Beef with Soy and Ginger Sauce

Makes 10
Preparation time: 25 mins
85 kcal/355 kJ

---

*300 g/**11 oz** beef fillet, cut into 10 cubes*

*salt and freshly ground black pepper*

*30 ml/**2 tbsp** sesame oil*

*10 ml/**2 tsp** chopped shallots*

*1 clove garlic, crushed*

*1 red pepper, cut into 10 squares*

*10 button mushrooms*

*150 ml/¼ **pt**/⅔ cup red wine*

*60 ml/**4 tbsp** soy sauce*

*25 g/**1 oz** ginger root, peeled and grated*

*5 ml/**1 tsp** cornflour*

1 Season the beef cubes with salt and pepper. Heat half the sesame oil in a frying pan, add the cubes and fry for 3 minutes, turning. Remove to a plate and keep warm.

2 Heat the remaining oil and fry the shallots and the garlic gently for 2 minutes. Add the pepper squares and mushrooms. Pour on half the red wine and the soy sauce.

3 Add the ginger. Mix the cornflour with the remaining wine and add it to the sauce.

4 Bring to the boil, season with salt and pepper and take out the mushrooms and pepper. Spear them on to 10 cocktail sticks with the beef cubes. Cover with sauce and serve immediately.

**Gourmet Tip**
If you use pork, fry the meat a little longer so that it is well cooked through.

# Pork Kebabs with Tomato Sauce

Makes 10
Preparation time: 20 mins
115 kcal/480 kJ

*300 g/**10 to 12 oz** pork fillet, cut into 30 cubes*
*1 yellow pepper, cut into 20 squares*
*2 medium onions, cubed*
*salt and freshly ground black pepper*
*45 ml/**3 tbsp** olive oil*
*10 ml/**2 tsp** chopped shallots*
*1 clove garlic, crushed*
*3 beef tomatoes, skinned, deseeded and cubed*
*10 ml/**2 tsp** chopped fresh basil*
*25 g/**1 oz**/2 tbsp butter*

**1** Spear the pork fillet cubes alternately with the pepper and onion on to 10 skewers and season with salt and pepper.
**2** Heat 30 ml/2 tbsp of olive oil and fry the kebabs for about 5 minutes on a low heat, turning twice. Keep them warm.
**3** Heat the remaining oil and fry the shallots and the garlic gently for 2 minutes then add the tomato cubes. Fry for 5 minutes, add the basil and season with salt and pepper.
**4** Remove from heat and stir in the butter. Pour the sauce over the kebabs and serve immediately.

*Photograph opposite (top)*

# Stuffed Flaky Pastry Horns

Makes 10
Preparation time: 30 mins
210 kcal/880 kJ

*15 ml/**1 tsp** butter*
*150 g/**5 oz** ham, cubed*
*100 ml/**3½ fl oz**/½ cup single cream*
*3 egg yolks*
*a pinch of nutmeg*
*freshly ground black pepper*
*10 ml/**2 tsp** chopped fresh parsley*
*225 g/**8 oz** flaky pastry*

**1** Melt the butter in a pan, add ham and lightly fry for 2 minutes.
**2** Add three-quarters of the cream and boil gently until reduced to 2 or 3 teaspoons.
**3** Mix 2 egg yolks with the rest of the cream and quickly fold into the ham mixture. Remove immediately from the heat and season with pepper and nutmeg. Stir in the parsley and leave to cool.
**4** Roll out the pastry thinly and cut into small triangles.
**5** Put 2 teaspoons of ham mixture in the middle of each triangle, moisten the edges of the pastry with water then roll up. Shape into crescents. Transfer to a damp baking tray, brush with egg yolk and bake for 10 to 12 minutes in a preheated oven at 225°C/425°F/gas mark 7.

*Photograph opposite (bottom)*

**Gourmet Tip**
Flaky pastry is ideal for this recipe, but you can use puff pastry, which is readily available frozen in most supermarkets.

# Spinach Tartlets

Makes 10
Preparation time: 40 mins
190 kcal/795 kJ

*225 g/***8 oz** *shortcrust pastry*
*25 g/***1 oz***/2 tbsp butter*
*10 ml/***2 tsp** *chopped shallots*
*150 g/***5 oz** *spinach leaves, blanched and chopped*
*30 ml/***2 tbsp** *milk*
*45 ml/***3 tbsp** *single cream*
*1 egg*
*salt and freshly ground black pepper*
*a pinch of nutmeg*

1 Grease 10 tartlet tins with butter and sprinkle with flour. Roll out the pastry thinly and use to line the tins. Bake the tartlets in a preheated oven at 180°C/350°F/gas mark 4 for 5 minutes. Remove from the oven.
2 Melt the butter in a saucepan, add the shallots and fry gently until transparent. Add the spinach. Fry for a few minutes, turning.
3 Add the milk, bring to the boil, then leave to cool down. Whisk the cream and the egg and fold into the spinach mixture.
4 Add salt, pepper and nutmeg to taste and use mixture to fill the tartlets. Bake for a further 15 minutes. Remove from tins and serve hot.

**Variation**
These tartlets are also very good with a cheese filling. Mix 60 ml/4 tbsp of milk and the same amount of cream with 1 egg and 20 ml/4 tsp of Kirsch. Season with salt, pepper and nutmeg. Heat 40 g/1½ oz/3 tbsp butter with 45 ml/1 tsp chopped sage leaves in a frying pan until bubbling. Add it to the cream mixture. Stir in 150 g/5 oz of grated Emmenthal cheese. Spoon into the tartlet cases and bake for a further 15 minutes.

# Flaky Pastry Meat Rolls

Makes 10
Preparation time: 30 mins
170 kcal/710 kJ

*250 g/**9 oz** minced beef and pork, mixed*
*30 ml/**2 tbsp** chopped fresh basil*
*10 ml/**2 tsp** chopped shallots*
*2 eggs*
*20 ml/**4 tsp** milk*
*salt and freshly ground black pepper*
*150 g/**5 oz** flaky pastry*

**1** Mix the minced meat with the basil, shallots, 1 egg and the milk. Season to taste with salt and pepper.
**2** Roll out the pastry thinly and cut into 10 squares of about 8 cm (3 in).
**3** Shape the basil meat into 10 little sausages and roll each inside the flaky pastry, like a sausage roll.
**4** Transfer to a damp baking tray, brush with egg and bake in a preheated oven at 200°C/400°F/gas mark 6 for 12 minutes.

*Photograph opposite (top)*

# Lamb Balls with Roquefort Sauce

Makes 10
Preparation time: 25 mins
220 kcal/920 kJ

*10 ml/**2 tsp** butter*
*20 ml/**4 tsp** chopped shallots*
*10 ml/**2 tsp** chopped fresh thyme*
*300 g/**11 oz** lean minced lamb*
*1 egg*
*15 ml/**1 tbsp** breadcrumbs*
*20 ml/**4 tsp** milk*
*salt and freshly ground black pepper*
*60 ml/**4 tbsp** olive oil*
*100 ml/**3½ fl oz/½** cup dry white wine*
*150 ml/**¼ pt/⅔** cup single cream*
*100 g/**4 oz** Roquefort cheese, grated*
*10 ml/**2 tsp** chopped fresh parsley*

**1** Melt the butter in a frying pan, add half the shallots and the thyme and fry lightly. Leave to cool in a bowl.
**2** Work the mixture into the minced lamb with the egg, breadcrumbs and milk. Season to taste with salt and pepper. Form into little balls.
**3** Heat the oil in a fryin pan, add lamb balls an fry for about 10 minute over a low heat. Turn fre quently until evenl browned. Remove fron the pan and keep ho Pour off most of the oil.
**4** Add the remaining sha lots, fry lightly then pour i the wine. Bring to the bo and bubble gently until re duced by half. Pour in th cream, bring to the boi then strain into a clea pan.
**4** Add the Roquefor bring just up to the boi add the parsley and sea son with pepper. Pour th sauce over the meat ball and pick up with cockta sticks.

*Photograph opposite (bottom)*

# Index of Recipes



foulsham
Yeovil Road, Slough, Berkshire, SL1 4JH

ISBN 0-572-01706-5



Printed in Portugal